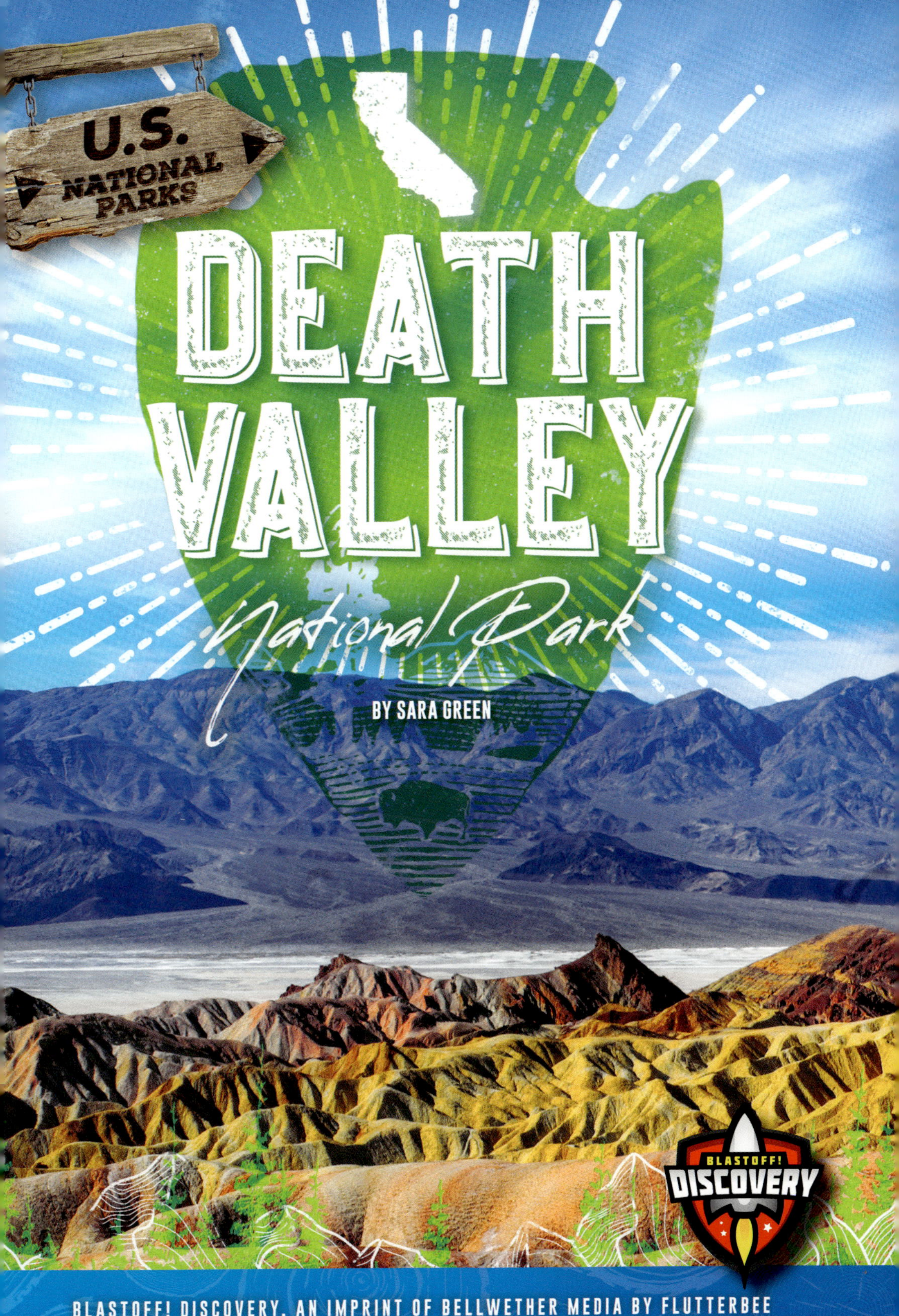

BLASTOFF! DISCOVERY, AN IMPRINT OF BELLWETHER MEDIA BY FLUTTERBEE

Blastoff! Discovery launches a new mission: reading to learn. Filled with facts and features, each book offers you an exciting new world to explore!

This edition first published in 2026 by Bellwether Media, Inc.

For information regarding permission, write to Bellwether Media, Inc., Attention: Permissions Department, 3500 American Blvd W, Suite 150, Bloomington, MN 55431.

Library of Congress Cataloging-in-Publication Data is available at www.loc.gov or upon request from the publisher.

ISBN: 9798893048483 (hardcover)
ISBN: 9798893049480 (ebook)

Editor: Elizabeth Neuenfeldt Designer: Laura Sowers

Printed in the United States of America, North Mankato, MN.

TABLE OF CONTENTS

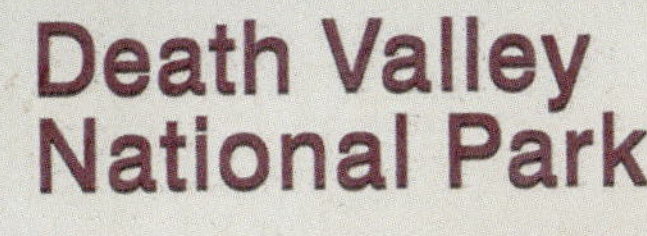

A SPRING ADVENTURE

BADWATER BASIN

BLAZING HEAT

Death Valley National Park holds the record for the world's hottest recorded air temperature. The temperature reached 134.1 degrees Fahrenheit (56.7 degrees Celsius) on July 10, 1913.

A family visits Death Valley National Park on a pleasant spring day. They are glad to be there before the summer heat arrives! Their first stop is Mesquite Flat Sand **Dunes**. The family climbs the high dunes. Then, they jump, run, and even roll down them!

Next, the family drives to Badwater **Basin** to see the **salt flats**. The white landscape spreads for hundreds of miles! The family ends their day at Zabriskie Point. The view is beautiful. At sunset, the mountains light up in shades of orange and red. Death Valley looks like another planet!

DEATH VALLEY NATIONAL PARK

Death Valley National Park is the hottest, driest, and lowest place in North America. It features rugged **canyons**, smooth sand dunes, and gleaming salt flats. Death Valley is the largest national park in the lower 48 states. It covers 5,270 square miles (13,649 square kilometers). Most of the park lies in California along the Nevada border. A small part enters Nevada.

Death Valley lies between two mountain ranges. The Panamint Range is to the west. The Amargosa Range is to the east. The mountains trap heat in the valley and make the area very hot and dry.

BONE DRY

Death Valley gets around 2 inches (5 centimeters) of rainfall per year.

BRINY POOLS

Pools filled with salty water called brine sometimes form in the salt flats. This salty water tastes bad. It is how Badwater Basin got its name!

Death Valley has some of North America's oldest rock formations. The oldest are at least 1.7 billion years old! Billions of years of **tectonic** activity, **volcanic** activity, and **erosion** shaped Death Valley's landscape. Earth's **crust** shifted and split along **faults**. This movement created the park's mountains and valleys.

Badwater Basin was once part of a deep, salty lake called Lake Manly. It filled much of Death Valley during an **ice age**. Over time, the area got warmer. The water **evaporated** and left behind massive amounts of salt. Repeated cycles of flooding and evaporation formed the salt flats.

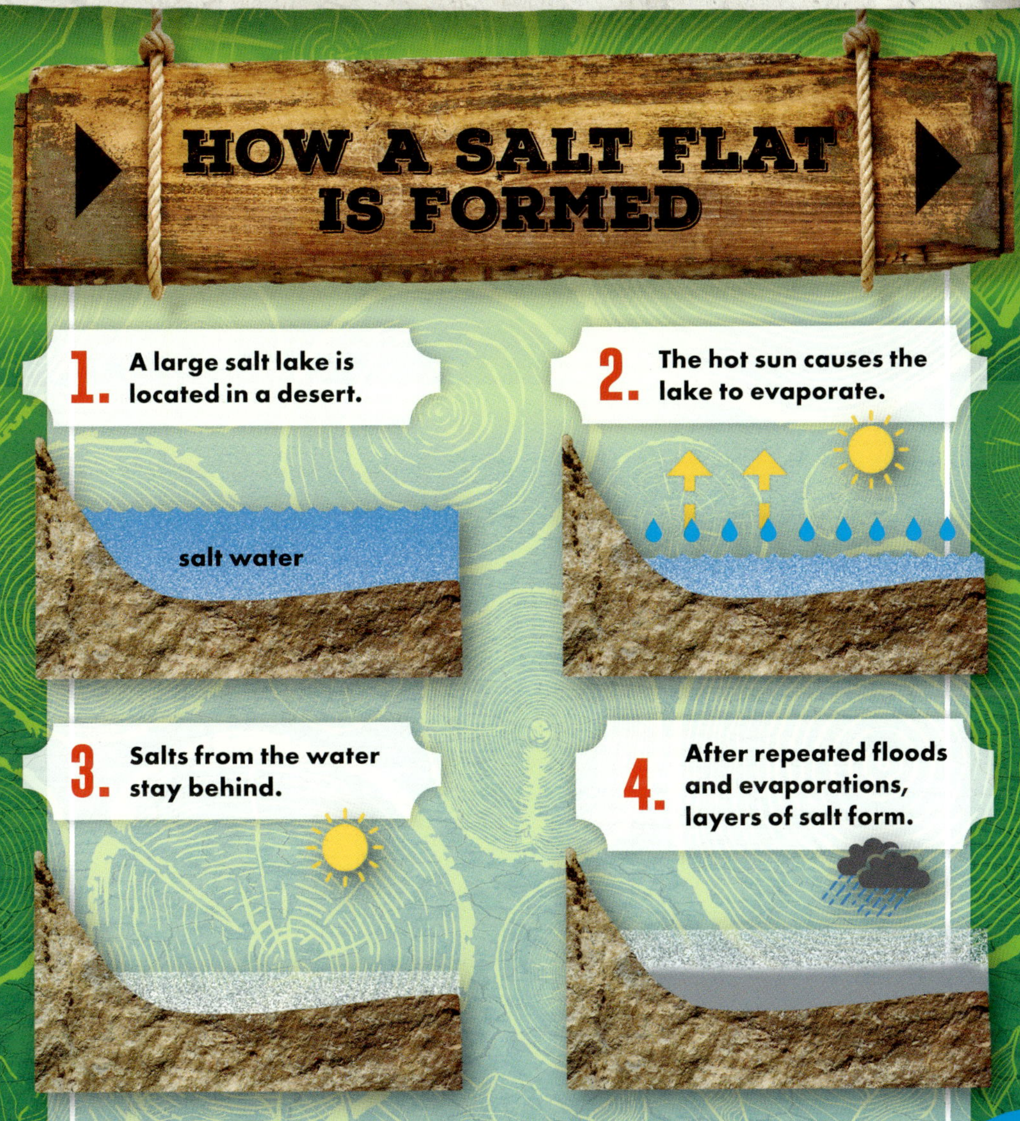

Telescope Peak in the Panamint Range is the highest point in the park. It reaches 11,049 feet (3,368 meters). A dry lake bed called Racetrack Playa is also located in the Panamint Range. It is where "sailing stones" are found. A combination of wind and thin ice sheets causes stones to move across the lake bed.

TELESCOPE PEAK

SAILING STONES IN RACETRACK PLAYA

Death Valley has four seasons. Summers are dangerously hot. Temperatures in the valley are often above 110 degrees Fahrenheit (43 degrees Celsius). Winters are cool, especially at higher areas in the park. Spring and fall are usually warm and comfortable.

PLANTS AND WILDLIFE

Death Valley is full of life! Across the valley, creosote bushes grow. Hummingbirds buzz around them and drink nectar from their flowers. Mesquite trees have long, deep roots to find water under the desert sand. The trees offer shelter for kangaroo rats and sidewinder rattlesnakes. Coyotes chase many animals, such as desert cottontails and roadrunners.

Mojave Desert tortoises rest in underground dens. This helps them escape the desert heat. Nearby springs are home to pupfish. Pickleweed and rushes grow by the water. Many different animals get the water they need from these springs.

CREOSOTE BUSH

COSTA'S HUMMINGBIRD

COYOTE

GREATER ROADRUNNER

PICKLEWEED

PLAYFUL PUPFISH
Devils Hole pupfish are among the rarest fishes on Earth. They only live in a salty, water-filled cavern called Devils Hole in Death Valley National Park. The tiny fish are named for their playful, puppylike behavior!
MOJAVE DESERT TORTOISE
Life Span: 50 to 80 years
Status: critically endangered
Mojave Desert tortoise range =
LEAST CONCERN
NEAR THREATENED
VULNERABLE
ENDANGERED
CRITICALLY ENDANGERED
EXTINCT IN THE WILD
EXTINCT

Higher up in the park, desert night lizards live in Joshua trees. Pinyon pines and juniper trees give shade for western skinks. Chipmunks hurry among the trees. Mule deer nibble on blackbrush growing along the ground.

SUPERBLOOM

Wildflowers in Death Valley only grow when enough rain falls. If the weather conditions are right, millions of wildflowers may bloom at the same time. This is called a superbloom!

MOUNTAIN LION

Life Span: up to 20 years
Status: least concern

Desert bighorn sheep climb the rocky landscape. They can go days without drinking water! They snack on cacti throughout the park and avoid mountain lions hunting for their next meal. Bristlecone pines grow in the highest points of the park. Ravens glide in the sky above.

HUMANS IN DEATH VALLEY NATIONAL PARK

Native American peoples have lived in Death Valley for at least 10,000 years. Some of the earliest people made carvings in rocks. Death Valley is the homeland of the Timbisha Shoshone. They have lived in the area for over 1,000 years.

Timbisha Shoshone **traditionally** moved with the seasons. In summer, they moved to the mountains where it was cooler. They returned to the valley in winter. The people hunted desert bighorn sheep and rabbits. They gathered pine nuts and bean pods. They wove baskets from willow.

The first white people arrived in 1849. They had gotten lost on their way to California to search for gold. After weeks of hardship, they finally left the valley and named it "Death Valley."

In 1881, a **mineral** called borax was found in Death Valley. Death Valley's first successful borax mining company began in 1883. It was later taken over by the Pacific Coast Borax Company. Around this time, miners also found silver and gold in the Panamint Range. Towns grew as more miners came. In the early 1900s, mining slowed and people began to leave.

MULE TEAM HAULING BORAX

A LONG HAUL

Mules and horses were used to haul borax on wagons. They traveled 165 miles (266 kilometers) over 10 days to carry borax from Death Valley to Mojave, California.

HARMONY BORAX WORKS,
A BORAX MINING COMPANY
STAY OUTSIDE FENCE

In the late 1920s, the Pacific Coast Borax Company shifted to **tourism**. They built lodges and offered train rides. Death Valley was named a national monument in 1933. This protected the land from mining. Roads, trails, and campgrounds were built. However, the Timbisha Shoshone were forced off their lands.

On October 31, 1994, the California Desert Protection Act named Death Valley a national park and increased its size. In 2000, part of the park was returned to the Timbisha Shoshone. They were finally allowed to live and practice their traditions inside the park again.

TIMBISHA SHOSHONE COMMUNITY IN DEATH VALLEY

VISITING DEATH VALLEY NATIONAL PARK

Today, the park welcomes more than one million visitors each year. Spring, fall, and winter are popular seasons to visit the park. Hikers can explore many trails. A short hike on the Natural Bridge trail leads to a massive rock arch. The Mosaic Canyon trail includes scrambles over rocks and dry waterfalls!

EXPLOSIVE EVENT

A volcanic explosion formed Death Valley's Ubehebe Crater around 2,100 years ago. People can hike around the rim and down about 600 feet (183 meters) into the crater.

NATURAL BRIDGE TRAIL

TOP SITES

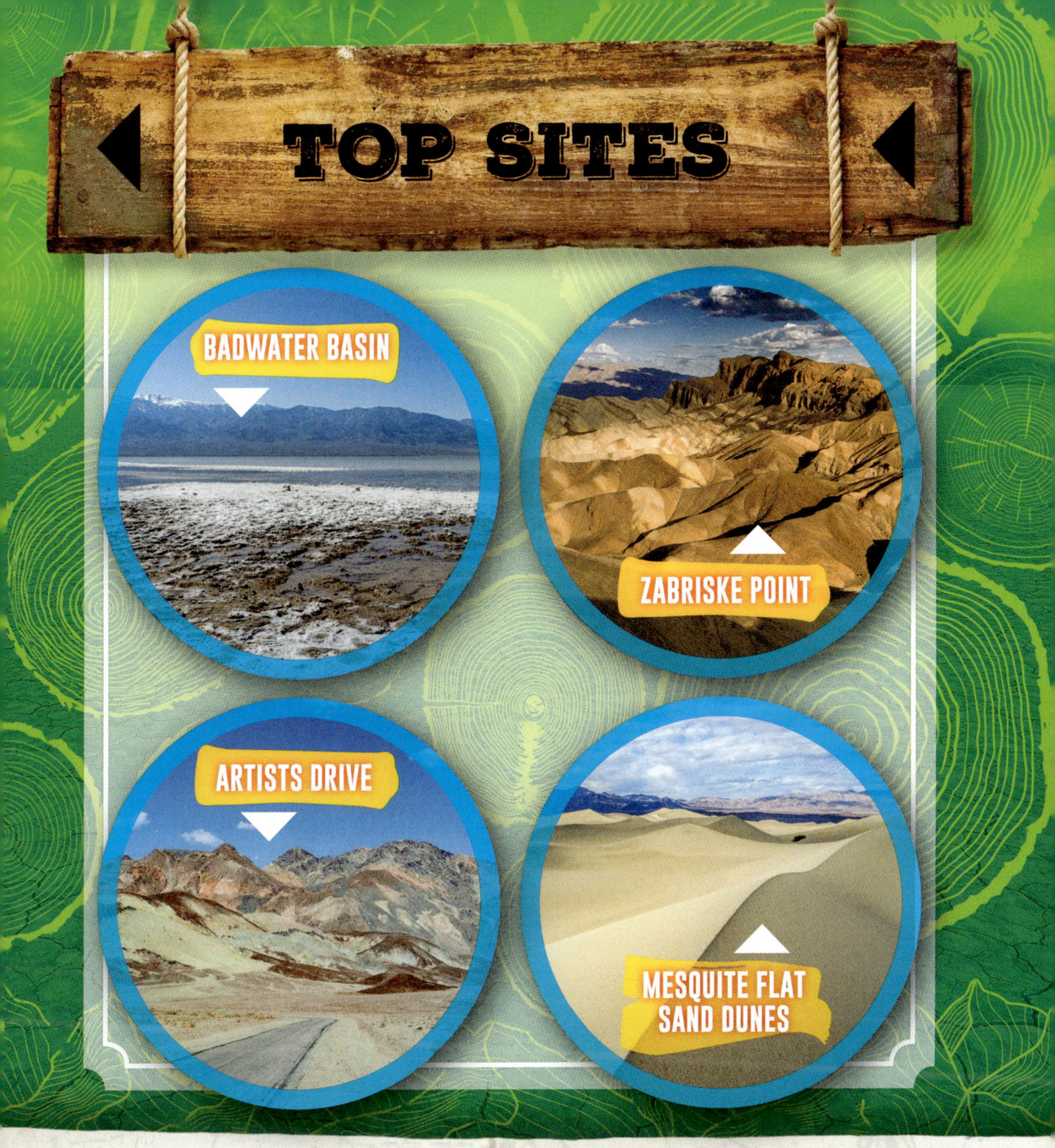

The Artists Drive is a 9-mile (14-kilometer) scenic drive. The road winds through canyons and past colorful hillsides. Harmony Borax Works offers visitors a peek into the park's mining past. Stargazers enjoy a display of countless stars in Death Valley's clear night skies!

PROTECTING THE PARK

Death Valley faces serious threats. **Climate change** is making Death Valley even hotter. It could become drier too. Many animals and plants, including Devils Hole pupfish and bristlecone pines, may struggle to survive.

Invasive species such as burros and tamarisk trees threaten the park's land and animals. Burros were brought to the valley as pack animals during the 1800s. Today, they compete with local animals for limited food and water. Human activity also affects the park. Some people drive their vehicles off the roads. This activity scars the land and harms plants and wildlife.

EUREKA DUNES

SANDY SONGS

The Eureka Dunes are known for their "singing sand." When the top layers of dry sand slide down the dune, the sand makes a humming or booming sound.

TAMARISK TREES
BURROS

The park's staff works to protect Death Valley. They maintain trails and remove invasive species. Access to Devils Hole is limited to protect Devils Hole pupfish and other wildlife living there. Scientists carefully track the number of pupfish. They also raise pupfish eggs to help increase pupfish numbers.

Visitors can help protect Death Valley too. They should stay on trails and avoid feeding wildlife. They should pick up their trash. Everyone can help Death Valley remain a natural wonder!

STAYING ON TRAIL

DEVILS HOLE

DEATH VALLEY NATIONAL PARK FACTS

Area: 5,270 square miles (13,649 square kilometers)

Area Rank: 5TH largest park

Date Designated:
February 11, 1933 (as a national monument)
October 31, 1994 (as a national park)

Annual Visitors: 1,440,484 visitors in 2024

Population Rank: 21ST most visited park in 2024

Highest Point: Telescope Peak; 11,049 feet (3,368 meters)

TIMELINE

MORE THAN 1,000 YEARS AGO
The Timbisha Shoshone arrive in Death Valley

1849
The first white people arrive in Death Valley

1883
Death Valley's first successful borax mining company begins

FOOD WEB

MOUNTAIN LION

MULE DEER

DESERT BIGHORN SHEEP

BLACKBRUSH

COTTONTOP BARREL CACTUS

1933

Death Valley is named a national monument

1994

Death Valley is named a national park and is increased in size

GLOSSARY

basin—the area drained by a river

canyons—deep and narrow valleys with steep sides

climate change—a human-caused change in Earth's weather due to warming temperatures

crust—the outer layer of Earth's surface

dunes—hills made of sand or other fine, loose material

erosion—the process through which rocks are worn away by wind, water, or ice

evaporated—changed into vapor; vapor is a substance that is in the form of a gas.

faults—breaks in Earth's crust that separate tectonic plates

ice age—a period in Earth's history when the climate was much cooler and large areas of land were covered in sheets of ice

invasive species—plants or animals that are not originally from the area; invasive species often cause harm to their new environments.

mineral—a solid, naturally occurring substance

salt flats—areas of land covered with a crust of salt left by the evaporation of water

tectonic—related to tectonic plates; tectonic plates are large pieces of Earth's crust that are slowly moving.

tourism—the business of people traveling to visit other places

traditionally—related to the customs, ideas, or beliefs handed down from one generation to the next

volcanic—related to a volcano; a volcano is a hole in the earth that erupts hot ash, gas, or melted rock called lava.

TO LEARN MORE

AT THE LIBRARY

Marcks, Betty. *The Shoshone*. Minneapolis, Minn.: Bellwether Media, 2026.

Oachs, Emily Rose. *California*. Minneapolis, Minn.: Bellwether Media, 2022.

Owings, Lisa. *Sailing Stones*. Minneapolis, Minn.: Bellwether Media, 2025.

ON THE WEB

FACTSURFER

Factsurfer.com gives you a safe, fun way to find more information.

1. Go to www.factsurfer.com.
2. Enter "Death Valley National Park" into the search box and click 🔍.
3. Select your book cover to see a list of related content.

INDEX

The images in this book are reproduced through the courtesy of: Oleksiy, front cover; Tom, p. 3; travelview, pp. 4-5; romanslavik.com, p. 5 (Mesquite Flat Sand Dunes); Nicholas J. Klein, p. 5 (Zabriskie Point); Michael K. McDermott, pp. 6-7; davidrh, p. 8; trekandphoto, p. 10 (Telescope Peak); oscity, p. 10; Richard Semik, p. 11; Jim, p. 12 (greater roadrunner); Felipe Sanchez, p. 12 (creosote bush); Melani, pp. 12 (Costa's hummingbird), 13 (Mojave Desert tortoise); Angel DiBilio, p. 12 (coyote); simona pavan, p. 12 (pickleweed); Olin Feuerbacher/ Wikipedia, p. 13 (pupfish); Tom Tietz, p. 14 (desert bighorn sheep); Phitha Tanpairoj, p. 14; Warren Metcalf, p. 15; Isogood_patrick, pp. 16-17; NPS Collections Courtesy Pauline Esteves/ NPS, p. 17; University of Southern California Libraries/ Wikipedia, p. 18; Kasbah, pp. 18-19; Christian B., pp. 20 (Gower Gulch Loop Trail), 23 (Mesquite Flat Sand Dunes); Unknown photographer/ Wikipedia, p. 20; Generic1139/ Wikipedia, p. 21; Alexey Stiop, p. 22; Tobias, p. 23 (Badwater Basin); Atmosphere, p. 23 (Zabriske Point); Comofoto, p. 23 (Artists Drive); Hladikphotography, p. 24; angeldibilio, pp. 24-25; Anthere/ Wikipedia, p. 25; Alexey, pp. 26-27; NPS/ Kurt Moses/ NPS, p. 27 (staying on trail); Dominic Gentilcore, pp. 27 (Devils Hole), 29 (blackbrush); Unknown author/ Wikipedia, p. 28 (more than 1,000 years ago); San Francisco Call/ NPS, p. 28 (1849); jun, p. 28 (1883); Hum Images/ Alamy Stock Photo, p. 29 (1933); Nick Fox, p. 29 (1994); slowmotiongli, p. 29 (mountain lion); scottevers7, p. 29 (mule deer); equigini, p. 29 (desert bighorn sheep); Oleg Kovtun, p. 29 (cottontop barrel cactus).